THE FICTION OF STILLNESS

The Fiction of Stillness

Robyn Hunt

Saddle Road Press

Saddle Road Press
Ithaca, New York
saddleroadpress.com

Book design and cover image by Don Mitchell
Author photograph by Delaney Covelli

ISBN 9798990054301
Library of Congress Control Number: 2024934138

No god is secure from the lofty flight of mortal thought.

— Sor Juana Inés de la Cruz

For those who have survived
and for those who have not

for Bonnie Jean

CONTENTS

I

II

III

I

The massage therapist, appearing more wrangler than gentle man,
whips his hands with pressure up and down my back,

my skin becoming compliant as pressed damp cloth. He seats
himself on a low rolling stool and takes my left arm,
tugs each bone and ligament sheath

from shoulder to thumb, middle finger, wrist, and wing blade,
then back to hip as if seeking electricity
in the river of pressure points

Mammogram in Pandemic

There is no pen, only this pencil from the clasped hollow
of what I carry to an outer room, square holding cell
with four chairs in their appointed corners like modern-day
stations of the cross,

separating the women in this pandemic, anxious for the procedure.
Busts pressed between paddle and Plexiglas. One wrist and one
hand raised to hold tethering metal, to hold a breath for the long
seconds

of shoulders unshrugged. It has been 12 lavish months
of unknowing since we previously waded in, praying
for nothing too fibrous or threatening,

no dark smudge on the film's flash in this recurrent exodus while
in our thoughts, we revert to youth when we had not yet
grown these globes and

future adoration of self emanated from two girlish hands cupping
nothing but gooseflesh. Instead, now, we reach for the bleached
ties attached to the sides of cotton exam gowns

with fading abstract patterns flapped and crossed over
in front like thin aprons, and the drink of anticipation
is thin swallow.

This pencil allows me to record and to erase, fill in the suspension
with notes to self. The occasional words I still cannot spell.
Curled ties like flaccid antennae which I loop in three pairs
of bunny ears and tuck

under the fold of my arm for this exercise, braced
at mammographer for silent hurricane weather to hit in low doses.
And one woman who has finished

bends to replace her black sandals, readjust her orange skirt.
Grips her purse of precious utensils to depart.

INTERFERING WITH SPECIFIC MOLECULES

The lobby is nearly empty in the hospital outside the laboratory
where I hold a single sheet of paper with test results
                    interfering with specific molecules

Grade II infiltrating ductal carcinoma with foci suspicious
                                    for survivorship

I make tearful telephone calls
                        My husband says he'll be there immediately

The table is smooth and round   *symmetric*   The chairs are
haphazardly placed at the end of this day   I have
breast cancer I say into the receiver

[communities must] pool resources

How to produce the sounds of the imaging   report into
sentences that resonate with months of postponement
weighty contrast on my right side

*computing and comparing IM ratios for greater insight
            not sufficient to prove the efficacy of screening*
      as if merely a coffee bean or moth wing

fibro glandular density and fear   *These two requirements are
necessary*

My hand presses down to smooth out   the leaf
substitute for film mammography
as if securing a place to nap   as if to fold the sheet into
a palm-sized sipping cup instead will push the breath back

This perspective includes the intrapersonal context

15

Then I realize there is a single stranger in a far corner of the room
all four quadrants examined

I whisper in his direction   *Bad news*   but I'm not even sure
he hears me
an individual's internal dialogue

yet as he rises to leave he wishes me one word *strength*
And the room unfolds   *between population groups*
entirely silent

I assure my husband I can drive myself home
recommended to search for correlates

I have known these avenues since childhood
the enhancing masses

I will follow the river and her tributaries
biopsies recommended
disparities in survival

SUSTENANCE

Wild overhang. No one goes here. Even rain is tentative,
brings down October and noon has little influence.

Blanched-bark tree pretends at green willow. Purple oval berries
strung above me on thin twigs wink in stippled sunlight,
mock sustenance.

I could crawl inside this shabby canopy where the house's
silver window screens are tattered flags,

long ago surrendered to high desert heat.
Fallen from their frames. Quietly cut away as if
night robbery.

Nature taking back. This washed-out chair
in the temporary shade receives my weight

Arms and legs let down as God's small
ants eat away at other trees and bushes, panorama
boxes of rejuvenation.

Here a dandelion spike so tall it has wished itself into a sunflower.
Nearby pink frill bells dangle on stems in enthusiastic spurts.

Growth where we had not dared to go until today.
Anxious path toward rest. As underfoot,
red leaves break into pieces.

SOMETHING SOLEMN PRESSES

up from under ribs like yeasty chemical rising
in the blue bowl that belonged to my grandmother.

In bed I lay my palms across the taut hillock,
ponder a baby breathing in the chasm

though this metaphor for embryo
is not healthy. Instead it gurgles, tight skullcap,

head clenched, a breathy moat surrounds
the fleshy prison beneath one unhealthy breast

and its mismatched twin. Were I to light a match
would the cavern combust? What perches inside

the sac around the lung? Or is it bladder pumped
full of remnant gin? Blowhard puffer fish

paddling beneath a sharp-cornered
raft of sour overinflated speech.

Heart on fire banging against tight corners.
Blackbird trapped in this ancestral bedroom,

frantic to get out, to find a rooftop from which
to call. Alien nugget and buckets of wishing

spring back as I finger this, my risen body bread.

DISPELLING FEAR: THE FIRE THAT BROUGHT THIS LAVA

tempted by the crevices between the world and not world
                                                    – Ada Limón

Lean toward earth, dear,
I think as I climb and
doubt my imperfect balance.
        Sharp is this lacey bedrock.
        Wash of former fire and
        loose-dirt skitter.

The tangle of worst imagined tilt
halts steady ascent. I grip
and angle toward the short sloped-roof cairns
and hardened lava fists to reach
        this precious pinnacle where colors oxygenate
        in clusters. Round-bellied juniper spreads
        bright olive on the ancient scarp.

With a single touchstone tangerine in my pocket,
sustenance for this craggy zigzag, I finally stand upright
and the rough haversack of old limitations lifts.

I exclaim in witness where we land,
      flotilla of fellow wanderers,
      who trust our guides and follow

to elevated apex,
to firm outcrop underfoot.
On the rock in front of us
        four coffee-colored turkey track
        petroglyphs and one
        six-fingered hand print as evidence

of a former inhabitant who also dipped from the waist
gathering distance in the middle of her day.

Fear not yet named drifts, then settles past avalanche.

Here we are in the box
canyon of breath's soft
bristle weed shock rising up
        through fissure
        and coiled beige stalks with eyelash tops.

And below this crystalline pigment of plateau
we picture the world before us
        a fired bowl
        perfectly finished
        black on black.

LETTER TO THE WOMAN IN THE RADIOLOGY ROOM

I am propped on this
throne of a medical chair.
You are here too, in the room,
reminding me not to move
as the radiologist maneuvers
the thin wires into my breast.
You at my left, handing him things —
coordinates and gauze.

Are you thinking of the shape of
the curl of your fingers on a keyboard?
Tremolo or legato. Of your son benched
for screaming at the referee? Of groceries
or the drive home, of dinner?

You touch my shoulder
gently, bringing us both back
into the chamber, where you have
placed a pillow behind me to make
this more comfortable. Maybe it is
your partner you are pressing
into the position, upright and still,
wishing that she would edge
closer, need you more.

Three guidewires are strung
like taut violin strings. Their spare
ends rolled into a coil
like a little braid of hair, and taped
down on the hillock of my anxious
prickly skin.

Maybe you are thinking of nothing
whatsoever but the routine actions
of the technician beside us. The light
like dusk, black and white,
on the monitor's prompt burrowing
toward the single small tumor.

Have any of your friends died
from this disease?

How did you arrive here?

Thank you,

Your patient at 1:45 pm

POEM IN WHICH I CONSIDER TELLING MY DAUGHTER THAT I HAVE
CANCER AGAIN

because two years ago my grown child felt safe
wrapped in her lover's embrace in the shower

bathed in early warm grief. The unknown, when first
I shared that my uterus revealed conspicuous polyps.

And today, a fresh carcinoma. Clip already inserted
to detect the new growth in my right breast.

Newly illumined tumor as much a surprise
as the number of disappointing attempts

my daughter has made to find a mate,
to secure love's assurance. As if latching on

to engorged breast of her insomniac mother.
Like this shadow on the slide. Her familiar baby fist

at rest on my chest beside the beating veins.
But what would be accomplished

in sharing this revived diagnosis.
Phototrophic branches blocking the sun

from the ground-crawling spines of spiked holly.
I retreat outdoors to trim the lilac bush,

slender, tall. Obstructing the entry address.
Blue number tiles on the wall hidden behind it

on the mud-brown pillar. I score and sever
the hardy green hearts

folded over on themselves to reveal there
a forgotten ceramic sketch of a single swallow.

My Safe Place

Here I am awash in morning tea.
Attempting again to translate
the language of cancer.
I will dress in healing yellow
or ambidextrous red. Will
carry each subsequent cup
to this crooked chair in the sun.
Journal each word revealed
at this time of no turning back
from future incisions.
I will hold my hands like reflectors
on either side of my face
determined to vacation with other
future survivors whose pleasure
darts here in the morning air.

II

The masseur comes around the table to my right side and lifts
again the weight of my appendage drape. I clench slightly with

muscle memory of discolored incisions along my right breast
and underarm. Malignancy lifted like a fisherman engaged

in acquisition, hook and tug, sentinel nodes mined like watery
black pearls. I remember being told that tattoo ink can leak

into the glands, slow poison, and spill
like tinta de calamar when sliced.

Flight

1.

Two broad ACE bandages circle my chest, pinker
        than my skin, as if female stowaway seeking to pass.
Compression against the incision where the tumor
        has now been plucked out. My hair pressed patiently

into French braids which I will not wash for three days
        saving the surgeon's opaque glue and momentarily
dry notch.
        Future pucker as memento.

Staff have read the inner insignia and confirm that all margins
        are clear of remnant cancer, my recurrent nemesis.

2.

Shuttered bird caw duller now than the lyric that first called
        her out. Tomorrow the sun will find me
fondling the weight of precious *milagro* around my neck.
        Pounded silver icon of a breast with darkly centered nipple.

Under protective promise from my daughter, this jagged course
        of perseverance. I will press
on with nuclear medicine processed by a man I imagine in a lab
        coat in the nearby hills, a former friend, who suffered
a stroke and abandoned the more deadly weaponry to
        coax chemical properties from the atoms'

molecular activity to pinpoint and to heal.
        As bandages, as witness, cut softly into skin.

3.

In preparation, technicians etch small tattoos barely detectable
        on skin. Make a map of my chest and underarm
for next steps. Belt of constellation. Four stretched corners.
        Pinprick stars.

My arm above my head, again. My weakening logical thought.
        The invisible piercing, external beam.

4.

In two years, I will deftly drink between subsequent
        mammograms. Over supper or lunch, rarely touch
the long scar along
        the right breast's droop.

Will knowingly greet the sturdy jewelry of
        miracle memory on a chain on a hook in the bathroom.
Like the memory of my daughter's placenta
        itself an amulet and ritual burial under a strong beanstalk

evergreen in a yard where we no longer live
        as I breathe the recurrent nightmare of fear
withdrawing finger nails and broken light bulbs from
        gritty dirt

and advise my grown child too to let out each breath
        she's held so long through her mother's testing.
She who lulled me to sleep the night before each procedure
        with the very lullabies I once sang to her

of edelweiss and blackbird singing in the dead of night.

PORT

I take to the porch. The sun
my most reliable companion.

My daughter sang lullabies again
to me last night.

White floral fists of comfort
squeezing me to sleep.

Waking, I recollect picking
blackberries with my little sister.

Brushing our daring knuckles
between bramble and thorn scrape.

Today I boil eggs for dyeing.
Hard shells show cracks

in their nest of sizzling water.
Nearly Easter and I long to find

the wafer-thin chocolate coins tucked
inside their gold foil wrap.

But plastic glue this morning is scratchy
icing on my chest incisions.

The chemo port's three-pronged star
like a tiny pill-bottle stopper pressing
against the skin from the inside.

Hidden hummingbird egg.
Tomorrow's discovery, since insertion,

will be sunrise mottled cackleberry,
bruise or badge between clavicle and

rise of the uncompromised.

Lightweight Valuables

after George Oppen

If I cut my hair,
approaching

chemotherapy,
let's refer to it as

fruit-tree blossom
scatter — anticipatory

lightweight
valuables

cautiously
chosen

windy decision-
making ahead

CHEMO CHAIR

When I first arrived in this upstairs room of three dozen La-Z-Boy
recliners, I brought a molded red heart with holy sand pressed

inside. Here then was a wide lap in which to rest. Chair as respite
and odd altar.

I lift my face and repeat my full name and birthdate. Tote
prerecorded music and cold pineapple to eat with a tiny shrimp
fork.

Chair as concession stand. Front-row seat. Monday morning
times twelve.

My daughter, my plus-one at this grim party, says to me, *Mom,
never place sacred objects on just any surface, but on top of
something that belongs to you.*

Tie-dye bandana. Two-inch plastic Battle Beast raccoon
little warrior fist raised to ward off danger.

As the time passed it was not the brightly lit front room that
I gravitated toward but the back corner that nurses referred to

as the dungeon, behind a private door, familiar now, with
a sturdy beige patient receptacle on wheels tucked inside.

Upholstered meditation instructor. I am eased into treatment
submission. Volunteers arrive with foot massage, red apples,
and forbidden Nutty Buddy bars.

Eventually I can smell the difference between silent infusions.

Taste the antibiotic, the IV push pre-chemo that is Pepcid and dexamethasone burning in the groin. Anti-nausea defense.

No-man's-land. Prescription chair. Room like an airplane fuselage of white noise. Travelers in temporary erasure. Stewardess nurses in soft blues shuffling.

Dressing Up Anxiety

Cannot settle. Cannot sleep.
One nurse speculates the culprit is
a steroid administered for nausea.

My mouth so dry I rub my tongue
and fingers over my teeth
in an attempt to recall them,

to release the slick and the rough.
Today we shear my clumping hair
close to my scalp. Bristles catch at night

against the dark-sky pillowcase

but my radiation oncologist exclaims
how colorful I am in evergreen cap and
orange beaded earrings, black T-shirt

studded with butterflies. I feel alive
in this momentary compliment,
this short meeting about modern medicine.

As if reading lines for the upcoming drama,
a frightening part that belongs to another.

Whisper Prisoner

I read from a memoir manual
with paper and pencil ready.
The stereo hums remotely. Hail begins

to hit hard against the skylights.
In one subtle blur-click everything
shuts off.

I dredge sideboards for candles,
find long-forgotten flashlights, make
temporary altars of the table

and counter. In the back bedroom
my husband, none the wiser, is suspended in a nap.

The dog disappears into the bathroom,
eying the slick bathtub as if she might crawl
inside.

The storm is that loud.

Detectors emit pitchy chirps, untethered
from their original power source. I imagine ice melting
in the freezer and milk going sour.

I carry cartons outside in the dark.
It seems sensible then to build a fire
in the fireplace.

The fiction of stillness makes itself at home.
Sparking and spitting. Persistent rain
seeks what is snapped or broken.

I hold a tiny sphere of light in front of me.
Enter the hall, the next room, and the next,
reassuring the dog that quiet will return.

Come morning, we are like children again.
I tell the sleepyhead everything he missed.

We are secure now in our single cave
of blankets, fabricating volumes from runoff
and slick pavement.

We stitch together survival windows and doors,
take whisper prisoner for future reservoir.

Animals in the Bloodstream

The nurse who checks my blood pressure
on the second floor of the chemo ward
cannot pronounce my last name.

She removes the tight cuff from my arm
and asks me an odd question.
"What is your relationship to horses?"
as if more psychic than RN,
plucking coarse hair from air.

All I can recall in that moment is childhood:
buckskin mares and muscled geldings milling nearby
with their sticky hay and bare backs as I floated
in a silver horse trough in Oklahoma.

And two fillies that stood sleeping behind our house
on Cerro Gordo, between concrete shuffleboard
and crumbling adobe fence abutting
the narrow, often icy New Mexico river.

But there was no equestrian therapy
in either of these interactions. No horse
here in the room with me today but maybe
our black herding dog that we recently put down,

nudging me now toward recovery.

"Horses are associated with healing,"
the nurse goes on to tell me as she completes
her task and gathers up her tools to depart.

I tell her I will keep a lookout. Then she is off,
softly forming the name of her next patient
on her tongue, life in a chart in her hands.
Animals in the bloodstream.

The toxins begin to drip into the port
below my neck, smoky tubing
like leather reins resting lightly on one shoulder.
I think of award ceremonies. Of horseshoe

wreaths of roses around the neck of triumphant
racehorses tethered to their jockeys.

And for a moment, I find myself missing
the ponies of my early life and wishing
for a Shetland with scraggly mane
to hang on.

To coax in tentative, prescribed circles
in a paddock, tethered to a more certain
center as I ride peacefully, gripping pommel
and curiously tangible air. Greeted with warm
wet breath in my outstretched cupped hands.

HUNTER-GATHERER

for Art

See the mushroom hunter-
gatherer as she scoops up
the cups that will be ground

spooned into capsules
to treat me. Immune boosters,
warrior shiitake

hen-of-the-wood and turkey
tail. A dose of lion's mane
for memory. Amber palettes, these

sorcerers' cheeks. Ringed as the tree
foretelling long lifespan. Feather
edges resembling oyster shell.

Bulb of ebony ears singing
from motherly mycelium.
Forager's tangle under ground.

Cancer patient's trust fund.
Loam of my right breast.
Others risk colon, brain, prostate

throats begging for respite
from radiation, from chemotherapy.

Mix this instead: tumor tea,
or two tablets daily to more clearly
remember

when we stood on the city steps
reciting Dickinson and Kerouac
on buses and in the park,

readied to watch the sun sink
or rise at Land's End. Psilocybin,

hope in a magical gel wrap.
Hand on the earth. Anxiety
tamer. Whisper in the ear.

BLING

Yesterday my echo-scan tech
was Alexis in a white coat
with eight lapel pins, encrusted
silver fleur-de-lis and rhinestone
butterfly, brooch of cubic zirconia
I imagine I would have found
on my grandmother's nightstand
fifty-two years ago.

"Undress from the waist up,"
she advises, "gown open to the back."
This but one of half a hundred gowns
I've worn this year. Today an action
photo of my heart, measuring muscle
to monitor the effects of medicine
meddling with protein,
cancer's appetizer.

Her canvas, my left breast and the arch
in my throat where I swallow.
"Put your left arm above your head
as if preparing for a nap."

I hold my breath on inhalation so that
the diaphragm can move away for
better viewing. Sound wave unable,
she explains, to pass through air or bone.

As the pandemic still restricts, we both
wear masks closed at the bridge of our nose.
Disguising mouths and preventing
smiles from escaping. I hear the wash
of beating, of my valves' persistence.

Eleven weeks in for chemo,
one week out. This hospital and its
sister clinic soon to become merely
those buildings that I point to:
there is where my daughter was born, I'll say,
and there I shared a room with cancer's
conqueror. Badges for entry, the surgical slits.
Endurance's gold necklace and heavy watch.

Through both visitations I could have easily
slept, as today, while my heart maintains
its familiar tasks. Alexis's transducer
moving across flesh like a divining rod.
Pillows under my head
and legs like foreign animals
in yet another conversation with patience
splayed on a mechanic's table,

passive to the passage of sound bouncing
in this necessary recital of the body
under another's hands. Electrodes on my chest,
temporary bling.

Picture Window

Six women arrive at the table. We cup lingering insomnia and
remnant dreams in crowded dissipating wisps,

confusing directions and faceless men. We arrive to decipher.
Mouth groggy snippets over biscuits and bacon. Outside, snow

releases its own sigh. We've each returned to previous seats.
Forks placed to the left or tossed collectively into the center.

Last night we drank here over Scrabble tiles, assembling nouns.
Making up rules. Dwindling moons. Now, one early riser

emerges from this day's weather. Sock monkey with down
on her brown cap. We start a new game.

Acronyms are not acceptable, we decide, directions nowhere
to be found. I patiently steep my drink. One undresses to hot tub

on this vacation patch of Colorado cottonwood and pine.
Red cars wearing white in the driveway. We mouth the names

of bygone partners. How we arrived here. Fortunes printed
on our tea-bag tags. The crowded world on the other side

irrelevant. One whips fresh eggs by hand to a froth. As we stir
words take shape.

III

On the massage table I loosen all filaments of connection
to the past where decisions have already been made.

Befriend a self-imposed suspension like turning

pages in my sleep. Imagining right thumb as weight, and forefinger
nimble digit – bending toward contemplative lifting

as another's hands fidget and predict. Foraging muscle.

My own hands finally at rest at my sides.

MADE VISIBLE

The yard is swathed in blossoms.
Ornamental plum comes full circle,
its leaves like rewrites
discarded

to this season with pale burgundy
droplets falling. As if to sound
the breath's arterial thread
through the body's old canals.

This honey-powder hint. Responsive in breeze.
Transparent feeder empty against the tree
where holiday lights remain in sunlight.
Spark of what comes next.

Crab apple or apricot. Promise of my patient
daughter. Her pockets.

Yet as I watch this morning there is
no one out there and no picking yet
except to spy the subtler pigments —
pink and white and hint of tan

peering from the tips of tributary limbs.
One branch my husband has tied together at a bend
as if he knows something of grafting. Or simply

set out to repair what's gone absent with
brittle memory's revision.

Radiation Burn

Red Rover, Red Rover, send someone over. If it's my turn
first touch me on the shoulder. Lightly.

For my right breast is ruby rush apple and bruise blue,
a trampled corsage asking to be discarded.

I will not run quickly into anyone's arms today
or be bully-whipped in play. Until

the wincing ceases and blisters subside.

Prizefighter's fist hidden, stained, an ache. Beyond
tired. Healthy skin cells recruited with cancer cells to die.

Rorschach test blotch. Fire ants. Sunburn after
sleeping too long on the beach. Stinging sand.

What Remains

When I turn on my side at night
I feel the pressure of sheet against scars

gall bladder gone and breast lump eradicated
thyroid's wing wrap long forgotten

ankle stitched back together with pins
uterus pulled through tunnel in pieces

As the surgeons whittled away, flakes of history
entered my anesthetized bloodstream and departed

leaving the body drenched, the body clearing

what is left after the organs are used up or taken
absence indescribable to onlookers

bruises rising from beneath, under cloth
to puddle like handprints after the cutting

I record each disappearance from my narrowing desk
this frightened conversation logged

Feeling returns to the slit places where soft tissue is knotted
like worry stones of the mortal and palpable body

In the morning I raise the blinds in the study to see the trees
leafless skeletons coming through the skin of sight
scratchy against the grey sheet of sky

I befriend the persistent stalk of sunflower
expiring in the backyard, head tilted to earth

I will snip each stubborn seed from the husk
to bury in the bed   to bring dreams back

I hold my breast in my hand like a baby bird fallen
body still warm and thrumming   it summers here
in this beaker of oncoming winter inside the emptying
reliable house

APPLES AND OATMEAL

Greens once grew alongside
our Cuyamungue doublewide.
Mint for digestion and chamomile
for baby's croup, colic, and fever.

Had I been a more discerning
collector, I would have cupped
clippings for transport,
transplants for the future.

I dilute apple-cider vinegar.
Soak my arthritic hands,
gargle against a throat raw
with the seasonal cold.

Cherry-juice concentrate poured
into a welcoming glass
when chemotherapy drip
temporarily took taste away.

My stomach aches and my husband
makes me oatmeal with red apples
chopped into small cubes
as my grandmother did.

I stir the same rolled oats into a bath
against the urge to scratch
flattened berry chicken-pox flare-ups

or bites acquired running through summer.
Berries, lemons, and cacao —
flavonoids bring back lust.

After Completing Twelve Weeks of Chemo, I Retreat to a Ghost Town in Colorado

1.

From my third-floor bed-and-breakfast window I observe a man
arranging lawn mowers for rent on the asphalt.
Spraying them down with a hose. Cars slide past.
There are countless ways to describe each auto's sound soaring
through this town, population 266.
Coasting to the gas station at one end of Main Street
or revving toward mountain altitude at the other.
A grumble of weight. Teaspoon of exhale. Strum
of a ghostly guitar. Applause like playing cards in spokes,
like autumn arriving in trees.

Third-graders run past below with Independence Day
pinwheels. Generations of wind. Mothers saunter on the sidewalk
with one last cigarette.

2.

Sunday church services close and village folk and visitors scurry
to the liquor store. Bicycles glide to squeaky stop at the Farmers'
Market, a single produce truck in an empty lot.
Inhalation of lemon, sigh of basil.

From a makeshift dispensary on the tailgate
of a turquoise truck, beer escapes from taps.

3.

There is a hint of fire
erupting at any time.

I know my treatment infusions are not entirely over but today
I rest in this rented chair with my feet up and hear a kettle
simmering, another's lullaby hum.

One traveler, oblivious to enchantment, tosses a can
from his car window — contrail trajectory laid close to the ground,
comes to a slow halt with a lit firecracker sizzling inside.

Up to the Elbows

I remove my leaden wings.
Replace them with survivor scalp
of post-chemo down.

Speak to the angels in my sleep. Assure
my daughter I will always catch her.
What I've grown from such compost

is splendor. What I chant still are the ABCs.
Washing my hands and arms
up to the elbows.

ÉTUDE

God is in the room   so blue   no single piece of art   other than
the performer poised before the fallboard and the grand piano
glinting with its lid raised

I enter stilled river and settle in a straight-backed chair with give
where there are only windows   hammers   strings   keys   inside
moving clouds   hammock shadows

River, never mind the shoulders of rocks   this mechanical
memory of wippen spoon and flank at rest   I am a girl again
feet released from practice   from pedals that damp

I murmur the recognizable étude   run alongside the brook
face in sun   songbird of childhood's single precious green pear
on a blue plate

crescendo of chestnut tinged with silver I anticipate
smoke and nettles   yet find none   only treble clef then
ominous progression into

softly sliced steppes   scoop of sadness   lifted as his hand

teases out forgiveness agile as a mother's ten fingers at the bridge
watching from the window as her single daughter in the yard
balances morning invocation

full basket wholly restrung

before applause   and after this opening prayer
the pianist reaches in and sculpts   lace   chignon
history's certain story

child wading into water   past the bridge
past split-second vibration looking both ways for silver rain

so many years of practice   braiding supple tightrope
between hidden places

I can barely contain my hunger   pomegranate rush of blood
He bends the hush and carefully reveals the working hinge

HYMN OF BREAST

Oh to understand the symmetric
pleading of these morning mourning
doves' chatter of never quite
surrendering their hiding place yet
mewling directions. Desolate appeal
for partnership. Against the backdrop
of cars pressing through day's wind.
Other titters too of tinier tufts
and rustle departures. Nests
enmeshed in fat canopy of red
branches.

But this persistent pitch of
childlike toy train whistle is
the sonorous hymn of breast, of sun
dapple on blank paper. A direction
into the brush. Everyone is alive
this morning. The dishes are
put away. Pencil soft.
Crab-apple tree shoots sprout
from the base of mother.
Sole dove stills, her
partner gone momentarily
silent. Moving away, spit of a shadow
on the neighbor's parapet wall.

SCENT

for CB

1.

We tip our faces into yellow roses, rub bunched green
lemon verbena to release its scent into air.
Drawn in like hummingbirds or bees.

Then we cup, from a plastic baggie, grey ashes,
former body of our friend. The chalky sift through fingers.
We ladle ash over roots of cypress sentinels

and into monstrous tufts of blooming red rhododendron.
The base of tall pine. We imagine each entry she once made
into this park, passing children loud in their summer meadow,

to locate and inhale the sword tongues of sage. We mimic her
walking meditation as she unearthed her way from
an unfinished life to this redolent haven

foraging for her personal nosegay.

We trace ghosts on empty memorial benches.
Sprinkle this waterfowl pond with our sorrow
when no one is watching

where spiny backs of dark koi troll and breach,
fish that may have lazily swum in her direction
as if to acknowledge her weary sweat.

2.

We each tell a story in the fragrance garden
and cultivate laughter from a burgeoning dizziness.
Her intoxicating dust under our fingernails.

Night jasmine or stars. Afterward, I do not entirely wash away
the grit of her. Instead rub in the brittle remains. Her rupture
of poems,

her sight gone first. Then language.
These remnant flakes without scent. We make
our way back to our cars, heady with the cologne

of someone passing yet missing from our private olfactory
conversation. Pass a former shared residence in the avenues.
A façade once striped with purple wisteria. Bare now.

Broken Bits and Mending Tape

Sacred stones roll around on the floor of my car,
carried in through years of scavenging.

Pocketed. Parceled. Placed on dashboard
or grave. The sun bathes the windshield

and the secret messages written in mud or snow
show themselves for the innocent blessings
they are.

I walk into a café sounding with banjos.
Take the one free table against a window.

Squat wooden chairs are fashioned together
at the corners with metal,

corners rounded and smooth. As in
elementary school. When repair of broken
bits was as simple as binding with tape

MY FATHER'S EYES

What good am I sitting still?
I lean into the morning table
as if to support the weight
of my neck, sturdy board.

I am insatiable and wed to busy.
Taught to work and worry.
My hair has grown long again
wild as a mustang's mane.

Hooves hurling toward absolutely
nothing on the horizon but blue sky.
Deliverance in flying without care
for temptation that could break glass

and free the words I can't jog loose,
wrestling stillness from endeavoring
to become still. To say little except to
convey purely with my eyes

as my father does, relearning,
carriage weighted down less now.
Remembering the ornament of
one's center. Observation as keen as

cold, fresh water on high
mountain singing down, allowing
fish to grow, leaves to float,

and the wind moving across a bridge
that no one will immediately see
for its absence of need.
Its simple support underfoot.

GRATITUDE AND APPRECIATION

This collection unfolded in the gentleness of the kind and efficient staff of Christus St. Vincent Regional Cancer Center: my wonderful oncologist, Olivier Rixe, to whom I confided all things; the women in the infusion ward, who on certain days wore head scarves in solidarity with those of us without hair; the support staff, who provided blankets and snacks; and the radiation technicians, who counseled me to lie very still.

I honor my daughter, Delaney, with endless gratitude as she accompanied me to nearly every chemotherapy appointment and heartened my body and soul survival. I would be also be untethered from this earth without my mother, Kathryn, who was treated for breast cancer in the same year. And I grew stronger with the friends who brought cookies, stories, encouragement and unconditional love.

Thank you to my steadfast husband, Bob, who is always at the ready to read what I've written, to question and to praise.

I am indebted to the writing group with which I have been involved for close to two decades. Without their keen eyes and sensitive criticism, honing would be a much quieter and solitary act. These exceptional poets include Gary Worth Moody, Barbara Rockman, Donald Levering, Mary Morris, Tina Carlson, and Deborah Casillas.

Acknowledgment is also made to Dave Salhanick for his literary encouragement and our ongoing shared walk through the sustainable garden of our ancestors. And a beating heart to Evangeline. Always Evangeline.

For my publisher Ruth Thompson and designer Don Mitchell who endured my lengthy litany of questions, I am grateful for their patience and creativity.

And, finally, it was impossible to put these poems together without missing two vital women in my life, Bonnie Jean and Cathie Joan. I address then: May you be free of the ailments that took you from us as you romp now through Paradise.

About the Author

Among her former lives, Robyn Hunt owned a small bookstore in the San Francisco Bay Area and ran printing presses with a print and design collective, producing bread-and-butter jobs to enable the creation of poetry books and broadsides. While on the West Coast, she read poems with a cadre of smart misfits on the steps of City Hall and in North Beach drinking establishments. She was arrested at least once while protesting at the Diablo Canyon nuclear power plant. In the 1970s she attended San Francisco State University, studying Creative  Writing during the early birth pangs of slam and language poetry. Returning more than 30 years ago to her native Santa Fe, she occupied a New Mexico legislative press box as a reporter, and hosted ongoing readings and other literary events in a bookstore on Old Santa Fe Trail.

Her inaugural collection of poems, *The Shape of Caught Water*, was published in 2013 by Red Mountain Press and selected for award by the New Mexico Press Women's Association in 2014. Her other writing includes a one-act play, *In Possibility: An Imaginary Correspondence*, co-authored with Evangeline Brown and produced in Santa Fe by Theaterwork. Her work is also visible on her blog, *As Mourning Doves Persist*, and in various journals.

She and her husband live in Santa Fe, where she works as a development and communications director for a nonprofit social services agency.